A guide to the care & feeding of your planet

Earthwise
at
school

by Linda Lowery
and
Marybeth Lorbiecki

illustrated by
David Mataya

Carolrhoda Books, Inc./Minneapolis

earthwise

Dear Reader, When you write to organizations listed in this book, please put two first-class stamps inside each envelope to pay for return postage. Also include a note with your name and address on it. Don't worry if it takes four to six weeks for an answer. Remember, too, that if your friends and classmates all write to different organizations, you can share the information you receive (and that saves paper and trees!).

For my sister Martha Whitton and all those special teachers who open doors to roads less traveled.—LL

To Mom and Dad with love (for teaching me about the cheetahs and the fair-play-ahs and much more), and to Brigid McDonald, my friend and mentor.
—MbL

Special thanks to Curt Meine, author, researcher, and writer at the National Academy of Sciences. We also extend our gratitude to: Gaylord Nelson of the Wilderness Society; Karen Cornell and Arlene Strand of the Mountain Forum for Peace; Jerry Parks of Little Friends for Peace; Mary Eileen Sorenson; Debra Vezzetti; Michael P. Cahill of Students Against Vandalizing the Earth; Barbara Lewis; Bill Hammond; Designer Michael Tacheny; Jessie Lohman; Jill Braithwaite; Bets Pilon; Jenny Larson; Diane Hoo; Fiona Grant; Institute for Local Self-Reliance; Global 500; Greenpeace; Meridel Le Sueur Center for Peace and Justice; Minnesota Center for Book Arts; National Wildlife Federation; Native Nations; Rainforest Alliance; Solar Energy Research Center; UNEP; UNICEF; United States Institute of Peace; and the Wisconsin Department of Natural Resources.

METRIC CONVERSION CHART		
To find measurements that are almost equal		
WHEN YOU KNOW:	MULTIPLY BY:	TO FIND:
AREA		
acres	0.41	hectares
square miles	2.59	square kilometers
CAPACITY		
gallons	3.79	liters
LENGTH		
feet	30.48	centimeters
yards	0.91	meters
miles	1.61	kilometers
MASS (weight)		
pounds	0.45	kilograms
tons	0.91	metric tons
VOLUME		
cubic yards	0.77	cubic meters
TEMPERATURE degrees Fahrenheit	(subtract 32 and then) 0.56	degrees Celsius

Library of Congress
Cataloging-in-Publication Data

Lowery, Linda
Earthwise at school : a guide to the care & feeding of your planet / by Linda Lowery and Marybeth Lorbiecki; illustrated by David Mataya.
    p.   cm.
Includes index.
Summary: Gives facts about the planet Earth and suggests various projects and activities to help protect the water, air, and land from pollution and destruction, with emphasis on making an action plan for local environmental improvement.
    ISBN 0-87614-731-7 (lib. bdg.)
    ISBN 0-87614-587-X (pbk.)
    1. Environmental protection—Citizen participation—Juvenile literature.
2. Environmental education—Activity programs—Juvenile literature.
[1. Environmental protection.
2. Conservation of natural resources.]
I. Lorbiecki, Marybeth. II. Mataya, David, ill. III. Title.
TD171.7.L693   1993
363.7'0525—dc20   92-11221
                                    CIP
                                    AC

Manufactured in the United States of America

1 2 3 4 5 6 98 97 96 95 94 93

This book is available in two editions:
Library binding by
Carolrhoda Books, Inc.
Soft cover by First Avenue Editions
241 First Avenue North
Minneapolis, MN 55401

A teachers' guide is also available through Carolrhoda Books, Inc.

Printed on recycled, recyclable, acid-free paper.

Text copyright © 1993 by Linda Lowery and Marybeth Lorbiecki
Illustrations copyright © 1993 by David Mataya

Contents

Photograph Acknowledgments
Front cover: © Richard B. Levine; back cover: Debra Ernst, Arlington County Government; p. 3, © Frances M. Roberts; 5, 14, 17, © Richard B. Levine; 6 (top), Inter-American Development Bank; 6 (bottom), Colleen Sexton; 7, Judy Gunkler; 8, Lawrence Kolozak, South Coast Air Quality Management District; 10, Sierra Club of Ontario; 12, Rollerblade Inc.; 19, 33, Ohio Department of Natural Resources; 20, USDA Forest Service; 21, Western Wood Products Association; 22, © Jerg Kroener; 25, © David Julian/Rainforest Alliance; 26, Miranda Smith Productions, Inc.; 27, Utah Agricultural Experiment Station; 28, Wisconsin Paper Council; 29, Patricia Drentea; 30, © Arthur Morris; 31, US Fish and Wildlife Service; 32, L. Everett; 34, *The Kid's Guide to Social Action,* by Barbara Lewis, Free Spirit Publishing, Inc., Minneapolis; 35, Minneapolis Public Library and Information Center; 36, World Bank; 39 (top), JO1 Joe Gawolwicz, US Navy; 39 (bottom), © Paul Rome, Rome Communications; 40, *Washington Post,* reprinted by permission of the D. C. Public Library; 45, George Grall/ National Aquarium in Baltimore; 46, NASA.

What Does Earthwise Mean?

Have you heard about the bad things happening to the earth—oil spills, garbage piles, air pollution, poisoned rivers, and things like that? Don't let them get you down. There are things each one of us can do to make the planet healthier. And we can do them wherever we are —in our apartments or houses, our classrooms or schoolyards, our neighborhood parks or county woods.

First we need to find out as much information as we can about how the earth works. Then we will be able to take actions that make sense for the whole planet—actions that are *earthwise*. Sometimes these actions will be fun and easy to do. Sometimes they will be hard. There will even be times when it will be difficult to decide what's the best thing to do. But that's okay. There are always many ways to look at a problem, and it usually takes time to sort out all the facts and possible solutions. We often have to try a few solutions to see which ones work the best.

You and your classmates can begin your earthwise search here. Learn more about the challenges the world is facing. Pick a project for your community and get others to join you. Study all sides of the problem, come up with possible solutions, and work for improvements. Don't worry if change comes slowly. Learning takes time. We have a lot of learning to do to become more earthwise each day.

Cloudy Skies

More Than Enough

Each day there are about 260,000 more people living than there were the day before. For every one person who dies, four babies are born. We all add up, and there is only so much water and so much land on the planet. The water and land must be shared with all other animals and plants. The more people there are and the more we pollute, the less clean air, water, and land there is for everyone. Is there anything we can do? Absolutely!

We can learn about where pollution comes from. Then we can work to come up with earthwise solutions. We can also work to clean up some of the messes we've already made.

TOO MANY PEOPLE OR TOO MUCH WASTE?

Q: *Which do you think is harder on the planet—100 people or 1 person who makes as much waste and uses as much food, water, energy, and land as 100 people?*
A: *Neither. The 100 people and the 1 person have the same impact on the planet. An average of three times more babies are born in the poorer countries, such as India and Mexico, than in the richer countries, such as the U.S. and Canada. But in the richer countries, people generally use up to 200 times more land, energy, and water per person—through use, waste, and pollution.*

A NEW FACE ON AN OLD PLACE

Can a place that has been spoiled by mining be brought back to life?

Some Future Farmers of America in New Mexico thought so! These teenagers went to work on an old mining site near Raton. They built ledges and rock dams to hold water and soil on steep hills. Then they began to plant trees, grasses, wildflowers, and bushes. Their project, "Operation Wilderness," proved we CAN clean up some of our messes.

SKINNY BEARS

Black bears in Rocky Mountain National Park, Colorado, have been feeling the pressure of too many people. The bears are often disturbed by visitors and can't find the food they need. Forest fires, which help many kinds of bear food grow, are not allowed to burn in much of the park. Many bears weigh only half of what they should.

Kids from Louisville Elementary School are working with researchers to study the black bears. The children collect cans for recycling and use the money earned to buy radio collars for cubs. The collars help researchers track the bears to learn what the bears need to gain weight and live healthy lives in the park.

Breathing Hard

Since cities are so full of people, factories, and traffic, city air is usually more polluted than country air. On some days, people in large cities, such as Los Angeles and Mexico City, are told to stay indoors as much as possible. The air outside is too dirty to breathe. What is your city or town like? Count the smoke-stacks near you. Ask the factory owners what chemicals they put into the air and what they are doing to stop polluting.

A windy day in Los Angeles

A calm day

Stand on a street corner, and count the cars that go by. How many people does each car carry? Could these people get around town in a different way? Ask people in your neighborhood what they think can be done. Are they doing anything? Are you?

A CITY WITH BAD BREATH
In Tokyo, Japan, the air pollution is so bad that there are oxygen tanks along sidewalks. People who need a clean breath can stop to get one as they walk.

CITY HERO

Q: Who's that masked man in a red and yellow costume traveling down the streets of Mexico City?

A: Super Barrio. He used to be a boxer, but now he helps people fight pollution in the barrios—the poor neighborhoods of the city. He investigates problems, speaks out to crowds about solutions, and writes letters to lawmakers.

CLEAR THE AIR

How can you ask companies that pollute or harm the atmosphere to stop? Research the problem and solutions, and then write to the companies and ask them to change. Stop buying their products until they do. If enough people do this, the companies may decide to do business in a more earthwise way.

To find out more about specific kinds of pollution as well as the names and addresses of polluting companies, write to Greenpeace. Greenpeace is an environmental group that keeps a close eye on businesses.

Greenpeace
1436 U St. NW
Washington, DC 20009

POISONED PLACES

• An American factory in India that made insect poisons for farms exploded in 1984. The explosion and smoke killed 2,500 people. Many other people were left sick and blind.

• The Rocky Flats area near Denver, Colorado, contains some of the most polluted acres in the U.S. The army burned chemicals from leftover bombs there.

AIR TEST

How can you test the air you breathe every day?

1 Spread a thin layer of petroleum jelly on the inside of two wide-mouth glass jars.

2 Place one jar on a shelf in your classroom. Place the other jar in a safe location outside.

3 After one week, compare the jars. Which jar is darker? What do you think caused this? If either of the jars shows a lot of pollution, what are you going to do? It's probably time to do more research. Call your national, state, provincial, or city pollution-control agency and ask them to do an official test of the air near and in your school.

Ruining Rain

Some smokestacks pour out
tons of chemicals that mix
with raindrops in the clouds.
When the drops fall,
it's called acid rain.
Acid rain eats into the leaves,
bark, and roots of trees.
Insects and diseases then attack
the sick trees and kill them.
Acid rain spoils soil for growing,
kills lakes and rivers,
and harms ocean life.
What can you
and your friends do?
Become acid-rain scientists!
Collect rain and test it for acid.
Then pass your results on to
pollution-control groups
in your area.
For test kits, write to:

The Acid Rain Foundation
1410 Varsity Drive
Raleigh, NC 27606

SICK FORESTS
• *In the former country of
Czechoslovakia, entire pine forests were
stripped of their needles by acid rain. The
pollution was so bad that some people
had to live underground to stay healthy.*
• *Over 80% of the trees in Germany's
famous Black Forest have been
damaged by acid rain.*

NO MORE SYRUP?

Many sugar maples in Canada and the U.S. are dying from acid rain. Acid rain has burned little holes in their leaves, and then insects and diseases have attacked them. Without maple trees, there is no sap for maple syrup.

Where are the chemicals coming from? Large factories in northern New York State and other places have been pouring poisons into the air for many years. The clouds and winds have carried the pollution into areas where maples grow.

HEAVY METAL

When batteries are put into garbage burners, a mercury smoke is given off. This smoke poisons the rain, and when the mercury rain falls into lakes and rivers, it poisons the animals who live near or in the water. We can help stop mercury rain by avoiding batteries or buying only ones that are "99% mercury-free" and rechargeable. Bring all your old batteries to hazardous-waste drop-off centers.

SUN BURN

A solution to garbage burning and some of the pollution it causes has been found. At the Solar Energy Research Institute, garbage goes into a furnace that uses mirrors to multiply the heat of the sun 21,000 times. The heat burns up the garbage, and the ultraviolet rays destroy leftover poisons.

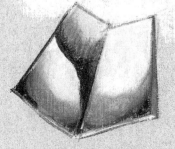

LET'S HAVE SOME LAWS!

Research keeps uncovering how dangerous acid rain and many manufacturing chemicals are to the earth. You can work to protect the air by writing to your national, state, provincial, and/or city leaders and asking for stronger laws against pollution.

Fewer Cars = Cleaner Air

Even if we could clean up all the smoke from factories, the air would still not be clean. Why not?

Because the exhaust from cars, trucks, and planes is one of the greatest causes of air pollution.

So what can you do about that? Plenty!

Walk, skateboard, bike, in-line skate, or roller-skate to places.

Share car rides.

Take buses, subways, and trains.

Make it a game with your friends and family to see how little you can use a car.

Keep track of your miles.

Try to go one or two miles less by car each week.

CITY SOLUTIONS

• If every two or more persons in the U.S. going to school or work rode together, we would save 600,000 gallons of gasoline every day. Think of how much less air pollution there would be!

• In Rome and Singapore, only buses, taxis, and bikes can drive into the city during the day. Car owners have to buy a permit to drive downtown.

• In Mexico City, drivers can use their cars only on certain days of the week.

• In Glendale, Arizona, the city will give city employees a bike for free if they promise to ride it to work at least three days a week for a year.

• In Boulder, Colorado, there are Bike-to-Work days. Prizes are awarded to the companies with the most employees riding bikes to work.

• In Denmark, most people use bikes to go to work and school. There are many bicycle-only streets as well as high gasoline and car taxes.

SAFE LANES AND BIKEWAYS

Many people don't ride bicycles to school or work because they are afraid of getting hit by a car. More people would use bikes if there were streets, paths, and road lanes just for bicycles. Many cities, states, and countries have started to build these.

Look at a map of your city or town. Are there safe bicycle routes from your home to school? To your friends' homes? If there aren't, you and your classmates can ask your city officials when safe bikeways will be built.

RAILS TO TRAILS

For over a century, train tracks have connected cities across North America. Many of these tracks are no longer used for trains. They are being turned into trails for biking, hiking, and skiing. Now you can bike all the way across the continent on train trails. If you and your classmates want to help in this project, write to:

Rails to Trails Conservancy
1400 16th St. NW, Suite 33
Washington, DC 20036

BACK TO TRAINS

Many cities around the world, especially in Japan and Europe, are using newly designed bullet trains and subways to improve transportation and cut down on pollution. The trains are convenient, move at high speeds, and hold many people at once. They are far better for the earth than airplanes, buses, trucks, or old-style trains.

Fuel for Thought

Why do cars, airplanes, rockets,
power plants, and factories
make air pollution?
Because most of their engines
or furnaces burn coal,
gasoline, wood, or oil.
When these fuels are burned,
polluting smoke is made.
Does that mean we have
to stop using engines completely
to stop pollution?
No! Scientists and engineers
are inventing new fuels
and new engines all the time.
These fuels and engines are
far cleaner and more efficient,
and they cost less to run.
But it takes a while to
change over to
these inventions.
Until then,
the best we
can do is use
machines only
when we
have to.

SUN CAR

*Did you know that some cars run on sunshine?
They never need gas. Their special engines
soak up energy from the sun's heat, and they
don't pollute. In Switzerland, more than 1,000
solar cars are driving around.*

THAT'S CORNY!

*Can you imagine an engine
that runs on corn gas? Or
a furnace that burns corn
kernels? Believe it or not,
these things have already
been invented. Corn fuels
and furnaces burn cleanly
and give off little smoke.
Ethanol, a fuel made
with corn, can already
be bought at gas pumps.
Corn furnaces are also
sold for homes.
Making fuel from plants
is not a new idea. In the
1800s, George Washington
Carver invented a vegetable
fuel that worked.*

RACE FOR CLEAN SKIES

Every April inventors race cars powered by the sun or electricity in Phoenix, Arizona. This race is the Solar and Electric 500. For more information on solar and electric cars, write to:

Solar and Electric
Racing Association
11811 North
Tatum Blvd., #3031
Phoenix, AZ
85028-1621

STUDENT CAR MAKERS

Each year Minnesota high-school students meet in St. Cloud for the Supermileage Challenge. The teenagers bring cars they invented to see which is the safest and most fuel-efficient car. Some of their cars have gotten over 200 miles per gallon on ethanol.

FAST, SLEEK, AND EARTH-FRIENDLY

Many car companies are unveiling new models of electric cars. One is the Impact from General Motors. This car can hit high speeds quickly, reach 110 miles per hour easily, and run almost silently. Because it is powered by rechargeable batteries, it creates no exhaust. And the car includes all the luxuries of a regular gas-powered car.

VEGETABLE CAR

Henry Ford founded the Ford Car Company, and in the 1930s he made a car out of vegetables. He wanted to show how farmers and industry could work together. The car body, which was made of soybeans, was so hard you could hit it with an ax and it wouldn't crack. The body was coated with a paint made from soybeans. And the car ran on corn fuel. Almost everything in the car could be recycled.

Tree Treasures

Cure for Warming Weather

One of the chemicals
put into the air when coal, oil,
wood, or gasoline is burned
is carbon dioxide.
Some carbon dioxide
is good for the earth.
But too much carbon dioxide
traps the sun's heat
close to the earth.
Then our climate
becomes too hot.
This overwarming is
called the greenhouse effect.
Fortunately, there is a way
to clean the air and fight
the greenhouse effect—
plant trees.
Trees absorb carbon dioxide,
and they make shade.
Every tree you plant makes
the earth cleaner and cooler.

HOW MANY TREES DO YOU OWE THE EARTH?

One North American scientist figured that by the time we reach the age of 80 years, we each owe the earth 2,000 trees. These trees would balance out all the carbon dioxide we put into the air from breathing, using electricity, and riding in cars. That number doesn't even count the trees we use up in wood and paper products.

If you start now, how many trees do you need to plant each year to reach 2,000 by your 80th year?

KENYA EARTH CADETS

Women's and children's groups in Kenya have planted over two million trees since 1977. Kenyan kids also work through the Wildlife Clubs to save wild plants and animals. To learn what they are doing, write to:
Wildlife Clubs of Kenya
P.O. Box 20184
Nairobi, KENYA

FRIENDS OF THE FOREST

After a forest fire on Soeharto Hill in Indonesia, 1,200 local Scouts replanted about 240 acres of trees. Every year the Scouts return there to camp, tend their forest, and watch their trees grow.

PLANTERS
FOR THE PLANET

You and your friends, teachers, and classmates can form a club just for tree planting. Plant as many trees as you can each year. For places to plant, call your principal, local forestry department, city park, or nature center. Plant a mix of tree types that grow naturally in your area. If you need information on getting free or low-priced trees for planting, contact your state Department of Natural Resources. Or you can write to:

The National Arbor Day Assoc.
100 Arbor Ave.
Nebraska City, NE 68410

HOW TO
PLANT A TREE

Here are some tips on planting trees:

1 Get permission from the owner of the land.

2 Keep the roots moist and handle them gently.

3 Pick a spot that gets some sun each day.

4 Dig a hole twice as big as the roots.

5 Hold the tree in the hole, and gently cover the roots with dirt. Pack the dirt down gently to remove any air pockets.

6 Water thoroughly right away and then once every day for the first week. Afterward water once a week, if you can.

Global Releaf c/o
American Forestry Assoc.
P.O. Box 2000, Dept. WM
Washington, DC 20013

Global Releaf c/o
Friends of the Earth
251 Laurent Ave. W.
Suite 701
Ottawa, Ontario
CANADA KIP 5J6

What Is a Tree Worth?

It's clear that trees
make our earth a cleaner, cooler,
more beautiful place to live.
But they do even more.
They give us wood for homes,
furniture, paper, and fuel.
Their branches
break the wind.
Their roots hold
the soil in place.
Animals use tree trunks,
bark, leaves, branches,
fruits, and nuts for food
and shelter. We use parts
of trees to make foods,
medicines, dyes, and paints.
Can you think of anything in the
world more useful than a tree?

A LEAFY INVESTMENT

Q: *You can buy a small tree for about $5.00. But what is it really worth?*
A: *If we add up the cost of everything one tree gives us in 50 years, it comes to about $192,000—almost ⅕ of a million dollars! That's what experts at the University of Calcutta, India, have estimated. Here's a chance to add up what one tree does in a lifetime and what it is worth:*

> Provides
> homes and food
> for wildlife
> *Cost to provide
> these things*
> **$31,000**

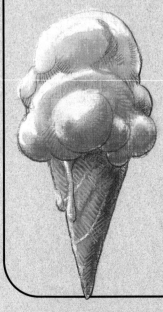

WOODY INGREDIENTS

Wood is one of North America's most important natural resources. The U.S. uses more tons of wood each year than all metals, plastic, and regular cement combined. The list of wood products goes on and on: lumber, plywood, pressed boards, window frames, cabinets, and countertops; paints, stains, and glues; rayon fabrics, carpets, Ping-Pong balls, and insulation; concrete roads, radial tires, photographic film, and parts of cars; chopsticks, telephone poles, and newspapers; boxes, bags, and books; etc. Even vanilla ice cream have tree products in them.

Makes oxygen
we breathe
*Cost to do this
with machines*
$31,000

Cleans air of dust,
carbon dioxide,
and other gases
*Cost to do this
with machines*
$62,000

Absorbs water from
roots, cleans it, and
breathes the water
into air for clouds
*Cost to do this
with machines*
$37,000

Puts nutrients
into soil
*Cost to do this
with chemicals*
$31,000

DIFFERENT TREES FOR DIFFERENT NEEDS

There are about 20,000 different kinds of trees in the world. Over 1,000 kinds grow in North America alone. Trees that grow naturally in a place usually have the best chance of surviving. Do you want trees that grow quickly? Plant cottonwoods, poplars, or silver maples. Long-living trees? Try oaks and hickories. Fruit trees? Plant apple or cherry trees. Flowering trees? Plant crab apples, dogwoods, or magnolias. Large shade trees? Try maples or chestnuts.

If you plant a mixture of all kinds of native trees, your forest will have a little of everything, and a variety of wildlife will be able to live there.

How to Cut a Tree

If trees are worth so much alive,
does that mean we should
never cut them?
No, or you could never
build anything out of wood.
But some ways of cutting trees
are better than others.
A bad way is to cut
all the trees in a forest at once.
This is called clear-cutting.
Clear-cutting leaves the ground
bare. The forest animals are left
without homes or food.
The shade plants that cover the
forest floor are destroyed.
The little organisms in the soil
that make a forest healthy die.
The wind blows
the soil away,
and the rain
washes
it into
rivers.

Avalanches tumble down
the bare mountainsides,
keeping new trees from growing.
If people replant the land,
they usually use only
one or two kinds of trees.
All the trees are the same age,
and they are planted in rows.
The forest has become a tree farm.

LEARNING HISTORY FROM A STUMP

If you come across a stump, count the rings. This will tell you how old the tree was when it was cut. Then examine the rings to learn the tree's history. The skinny rings were dry years, and the fat rings were years with a lot of water and sunshine. If you see black rings, those could be scars from forest fires.

There is a more earthwise
way to cut trees.
It is called New Forestry.
Loggers carefully select and cut a
small number of trees in a forest.
They leave the rest to grow.
They also leave old stumps
and hollowed out logs for animals
to use for homes and food.
Seedlings grow up naturally
from the seeds of the trees
left standing.
A natural mix of native trees
is often hand planted too,
to help the forest grow.
Then you always have a forest
filled with trees of different
kinds and ages.
New Forestry costs more money
at first than clear-cutting.
But it saves the forests
and all the life in them.
The soil stays rich, healthy,
and full of little organisms.
It is held in place
by the trees that have been left.
The wild animals have not been
chased away, and the trees
don't grow up in rows.

STANDING UP FOR A STAND OF PINES

Fourth graders in Marquette, Michigan, heard that the oldest trees in the state—the Estivant Pines—were going to be cut for timber. Some of the pines were over 500 years old. The students figured it would take $155.28 per tree to buy the forest. They started a fund-raising campaign that got other kids and people in the state to save the 80 acres of forest, one tree at a time. Because of the work of the children and the Michigan Nature Association, those white pines may now live to be 700 years old!

Shrinking Forests

If there are earthwise
ways to cut trees,
then what's the problem?
Most companies choose to clear-
cut forests because it's cheaper,
and there are few laws to stop
them. Forests around the world
are quickly turning
into tree farms or wastelands.
The problem, though,
is not hopeless.
Responsible foresters and loggers
are leading the way
by using New Forestry cutting
and planting practices.
How can you help?

Learn
about how
the water, soils, plants,
insects, fungi, mammals,
birds, and other living things
in a forest work together.
Talk to foresters and loggers.
Write to your government
leaders and ask for laws
that forbid clear-cutting
and encourage New Forestry.

*OLD GROWTH
HAS A LOT OF LIFE*
*An old-growth forest
contains many trees over 120
years old. Trees this old or older are
the best trees for many kinds of lumber. But many
wild animals, such as the spotted owl, depend on these
tall, old trees to live. Old-growth forests are also essential for
science, medicine, and recreation.*

*Unfortunately, these forests are being cut much faster than
they can grow back. To help save old forests, write to:*
Save the Ancient Forests
The Wilderness Society
900 17th St. NW
Washington, DC 20550

BIG TREES MAKE BIG ARGUMENTS

It seems that wherever there are old-growth forests, there are raging arguments. Should the forests be saved or cut? Some logging companies say that clear-cutting these forests will give people jobs and wood.

Other people argue that more jobs are made when some old forests are saved and New Forestry is used on others. These jobs come from selective cutting, planting mixes of different trees, researching the forest and wildlife, serving forest tourists, and selling hunting permits. Many logging jobs have been lost because of high-speed machines, high salaries for top executives, and overseas milling, not because some old-growth forests have been saved. The longer the forests last, the longer there will be jobs, wood, wildlife, healthy forest soil, and beautiful trees for everyone to enjoy.
If the forests go, so do ALL the jobs!

FALLEN GIANTS

***Q:** Where does one of the largest living things on earth grow?*

***A:** In the U.S. Some trees in California forests grow taller than the Statue of Liberty, weigh as much as 800 school buses, and live to be 3,500 years old. They are the giant redwood trees. These giants are being logged to make hot tubs, decks, homes, and fences. It takes two hours to cut down a giant redwood, but it takes over 3,000 years for a seedling to grow to its giant size of 20-to-30-stories high. To learn more about redwoods and the efforts to save them, write to:*

Save the Redwoods
   League
114 Sansome St.
San Francisco, CA
   94104

WILL THE WILDERNESS LAST?

Some forests and other places are specially protected as wilderness areas. Motors are not allowed in these wild areas because the noise, fumes, tracks, and traffic disturb the forest's animals and plants. Very few places are left in the world where cars, motorboats, snowmobiles, planes, motorcycles, and three-wheelers do not speed across the land. That is why these wilderness areas are so important to scientists and nature lovers. Wilderness areas are under attack right now. People who use motors for convenience want to bring them into wilderness areas. Companies that log, mine, or drill for oil want to use wilderness areas too. But if governments allow this, what wild places will be left?

For information about enjoying and protecting wilderness areas near you, write to your national, state, or provincial forestry department. You can also write to the Wilderness Society. (See "Old Growth Has a Lot of Life.")

Rain for Life

In some places of the world, especially near the equator, there are large forests that get a lot of rain— over 100 inches a year. These forests act like huge sponges. They drink up rainwater and give off moisture and oxygen into the air. The forests also take carbon dioxide and other gases out of the earth's air. Rain forests are so good at making oxygen and at fighting the greenhouse effect that some people have called them "the lungs of the world." Each day, though, thousands of acres of rain forests are burned or cut down for timber, farming, ranching, or mining. But if we want to keep our air clean and our planet cool enough, the rain forests must be saved. You and your classmates can help.

WORTH MORE ALIVE THAN DEAD

Just think of all the wonderful things that can be taken from rain forests without harming them: bananas, guavas, oranges, papayas, mangoes, and cupuassu (a fruit like honeydew); cinnamon, paprika, cloves, and black pepper; cocoa, sugarcane, peanuts, rice, rubber, and yams; chicle for gum, palm leaves for floral arrangements, and wood oils; medicines for cancer, high blood pressure, arthritis, and infections. Scientists think an incredible amount of medicines have not even been discovered yet. Whenever we buy things that have been taken from the forests without harming them, we help save rain forests for the future.

HELP ON THE SPOT

From Costa Rica to Malaysia to Java to Kenya, Scouts and Girl Guides are at work replanting rainforest trees. They may not be able to bring back the old forests, but they can start something new.

RAIN-FOREST FACTS

• 40% of the world's oxygen is produced by the Amazon rain forest.

• *The rosy periwinkle grows in only one place—the rain forests of Madagascar. It is used to make a drug that cures some kinds of cancer.*

• *North America has rain forests too—on the northwestern Pacific Coast. Thousands of acres of these rain forests are clear-cut every year. The yew tree lives in some of these forests, and its bark is used for breast-cancer treatment.*

• *Some rain forests are cut down to make plantations for coffee beans, bananas, cashews, and rubber trees.*

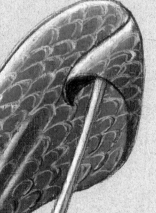

A CAN SAVED IS A TREE SPARED

Youngsters at Mililani-Uka Elementary School in Hawaii collected hundreds of cans for recycling. They used the money earned to buy 4.1 acres of rain forest in Guatemala. Many children across North America are doing the same thing. Other kids are having bake sales, puppet shows, candy sales, car washes, and garage sales.

To find out how you and your friends can join in the effort, write to:

The Children's
  Rainforest
P.O. Box 936
Lewiston, ME 04240

Save the Rainforest
604 Jamie St.
Dodgeville, WI 53533

To receive a booklet called How to Organize a Rainforest Week at Your School *(for a small fee), write to:*

Creating Our Future
398 North Ferndale
Mill Valley, CA 94941

RAIN-FOREST DEFENDER

Chico Mendes grew up in the rain forests of Brazil. To make a living, Chico and many of his neighbors collected sap from rubber trees (without harming the trees) to make rubber.

As the people started cutting and burning the forests for roads and ranches, Mr. Mendes spoke out against it. On December 22, 1988, he was shot and killed by some cattle ranchers. But his struggle to save the rain forests goes on.

Chico Mendes (pictured here with his wife, Ilzamar) worked to save the rain forests and his way of life.

MARKING THEIR TURF

The Awa people live in the rain forests of Ecuador and Colombia. They have seen ranchers, loggers, and farmers spoil their land. So they cut down a strip of the rain forest around their area. They use this strip like a castle moat to mark their land and keep intruders away.

It is working. Other peoples who live in rain forests are starting to do the same thing. These people know if the rain forests go, they will lose their ways of living and perhaps even their lives.

YOU CAN SAY NO TO TROPICAL WOOD

Common rain-forest woods are teak, mahogany, and rosewood. These are often made into front doors, furniture, boats, and musical instruments. If people refuse to buy rain-forest lumber, logging companies won't cut the trees. That's why some cities and states have passed laws against selling rain-forest woods. Cities or stores near you can say no to tropical wood too. Or they may decide to sell only tropical woods from companies that practice New Forestry.

TROPICAL WOODS NOT USED

WHERE'S THE BEEF?

Some rain forests are cut so cattle can be raised on the land. Where does the beef for the hamburgers you eat come from? Call up the restaurants, fast-food places, and grocery stores near you and ask them where they buy their beef. Are the cattle raised in the U.S. or Canada? Argentina? Brazil? Which countries have rain forests? Could the beef you eat come from cattle raised on land that used to be rain forest? Do you think cattle raised in North America is better for the earth?

When cattle graze, they eat the plants they like down to the roots before they move on. Heavy grazing keeps grasses, wildflowers, and new trees from growing. The unprotected soil can be blown or washed away. In North America, cattle often graze on public land—national forests and prairies. The cattle spoil the land for wildlife.

One solution to the worldwide cattle problem is for people to eat less beef. Less cattle could mean more forests and more farmland for feeding hungry people and wild animals. Another solution might be for North American ranchers to bring back the central prairies and raise bison instead of cattle. Unlike cattle, bison roam while they eat. Or the ranchers could raise cattle and move them every few days. Maybe all these solutions could work together. What do you think?

The Paper Problem

Many forests are cut
to make paper.
And over half the garbage
we throw out is made of paper.
That means we are busy turning
our trees into garbage!
So what can we do to change this?
Scientists and inventors have
discovered that paper can be
made from other things besides
wood: old clothes, algae,
sugarcane, hemp, and kenaf.
(Kenaf is a fast-growing plant
with woody stems.)
The quicker we stop
wasting paper and the
sooner we change to
making tree-less paper,
the more forests
we can save.

RECYCLE TO SAVE THE FORESTS

More than 500,000 trees are chopped down each week to make Sunday newspapers. Every year 74,000 acres of forest are destroyed to make mail-order catalogs. Over 800 million pounds of paper used in North America yearly is made from Brazil's rain-forest trees.

BUT every time one ton of paper is RECYCLED, 17 trees are saved, energy is conserved, and less pollution is made. Recycled paper can even be made into paper bricks that are as strong as wood. Soon we may have houses made out of recycled paper!

FROM BLUE JEANS TO PAPER

Believe it or not, you and your classmates can make your own paper out of old blue jeans and worn-out shirts. For directions, check out Paper by Kids, by Arnold Grummer, from the library. Or read Earthwise at Home, and follow the directions on page 19. Instead of newspaper, cut your favorite rags into tiny pieces. Or try vegetables— imagine carrot sheets or broccoli notepads.

PUTTING PAPER TO GOOD USE

Here are some tips for writing letters to government, business, and school leaders about an earthwise project:

1 Find out information on all sides of a question before you write.

2 Use one or two sentences to ask your questions or to explain the problem you are concerned about.

3 Explain your opinions, concerns, or solutions.

4 Thank the person for his or her time.

5 Ask for an answer to your letter, and give your name and address.

Dear Governor Robertson,

Did you know that every year many birds, fish, and water animals are killed because they get caught in plastic six-pack rings? I am very upset about this problem.

I think we need a law that allows factories to make only rings that are perforated or dissolve in water.

Please write back and tell me what you will do about this problem. Thank you very much.

Sincerely,

Keiko Oshima

Keiko Oshima
239 Azalea Avenue
Seattle, WA 98121

DRUG-FREE HEMP MAY BE OUR HOPE

Hemp is a plant that has the world's strongest natural fibers. Farmers used to grow hemp to make paper—as well as rope, nets, linen, canvas, burlap, and cellophane. The first draft of the Declaration of Independence was written on hemp paper. About 25,000 items that are now made out of wood, plastic, or petroleum could be made with hemp instead. Growing hemp, however, is outlawed in many countries because parts of the plant have been used as a drug—marijuana. Fortunately, scientists in France have just developed a new kind of hemp that would not work for marijuana. Maybe someday soon we will be saving our forests by planting drug-free hemp.

Sea Sickness

Oceans of Delight and Destruction

Over ¾ of the earth is covered by ocean water. Oceans give off moisture into the air, and sea plants soak up carbon dioxide. The oceans are home to many of the earth's plants and animals. But like the rest of the planet, the oceans and the life in them are in danger from pollution.

How can you help? Get to know your oceans. Visit an aquarium to learn about the communities under the sea. The more you know about oceans, the better you'll know about how to protect them.

AMAZING OCEAN ANIMALS

Did you know that sponges are animals—not plants? Or that dolphins may be smarter than people? Or that young albatrosses fly for several years without touching land? The more you learn about ocean life, the more amazing it seems.

NO SHELLS FOR SALE

Many animals that live in seashells are becoming scarce. This is partly because people collect shells to make lamps, wall hangings, and jewelry to sell. Many of the shells still have live animals in them, and they are killed to make art. This happens with sand dollars, sponges, and pieces of coral too. So the next time you go to the beach to collect gifts from the sea, make sure you're not taking home something that's still living.

WHERE HAS ALL THE COLOR GONE?

As the greenhouse effect warms the ocean and ocean pollution increases, many fragile animals and plants in the water weaken and die. Brightly colored shelves of coral off Puerto Rico's coast are turning white. This is a sign of illness. Scientists are studying the coral carefully to see if they can save them.

A KILLING SPILL

On March 24, 1989, the tanker Exxon Valdez leaked 11 million gallons of oil into waters off the Alaskan coast. The oil killed at least 36,000 seabirds, 1,000 sea otters, and 153 bald eagles from March to September. The plankton, fish, and other sea creatures that died can't even be counted.

Sixth and seventh graders from the Matanuska-Susitna School District went into action right away. They marked off three areas for study and then mucked through the oily sand and water to count all the animals and plants that were hurt or had died. They took notes, drew pictures, and collected samples. The information they gathered over several years has helped scientists understand how oil spills affect ocean animals and plants.

MYSTERIOUS DEATHS

Dead dolphins have washed up on the Atlantic coast of the U.S. Seals have been found dead in the North Sea. Whales are driving themselves onto beaches. Their bodies are filled with poisons from acid rain and ocean dumping. For information on what you and your classmates can do to save the oceans, write to:

Adopt-A-Whale
Tarlton Foundation
50 Francisco St.
Suite 103
San Francisco, CA 94133

Fresh Water?

Have you ever seen
a dead river or lake?
It's not a pretty sight.
The water is as lifeless
as a dried-up mud puddle.
No water birds. No water bugs.
Few or no fish —
just a lot of smell and slime.
How do rivers and lakes die?
Chemicals, sewage, trash, and
mud are dumped into them by
people or washed there by rain.
So what can be done?
Countries, states, provinces,
and cities can pass laws
against dumping anything
into the water.
People can stop using chemicals
on their lawns and in their homes.
Farmers can farm in ways
that hold the soil in place
and work without chemicals.
If everyone pitches in,
rivers, lakes, streams,
ponds, swamps,
and marshes
can be saved.

HEADING TO THE LAKE TO DEVELOP YOUR FILM?

Jeremy Lynch, a Canadian photographer, put a roll of used film in Lake Ontario overnight. When he came back, the film had been developed—that's how many chemicals were in the lake! He has also developed his film in the Love Canal in Niagara Falls and in New York's Hudson River.

LAKE ERIE CLEANUP

Twenty years ago, Lake Erie, one of North America's Great Lakes, was dead. The people around the lake realized something had to be done. They stopped much of the dumping of chemicals, sewage, and trash into the lake. After a lot of time, money, and effort, the lake came back to life. Some fish and plants live there now, and people can go swimming in it. The lake has a long way to go, though, before it is as healthy as it was. Lake Erie proves that people CAN change their habits for the better. But it also shows that it is easier, cheaper, and safer to protect a lake or river than to have to clean it up.

GOING GREEN TO SAVE THE RIVER

Students in 120 countries and at least 21 states are testing their rivers for pollution and sharing the results with each other. They are part of a group called GREEN— Global Rivers Environmental Education Network. For information on how your school can join, write to:

The GREEN Project
School of Natural Resources
University of Michigan
430 East University
Ann Arbor, MI
48109-1115

ADOPT-A-WATERS

What can you and your classmates do about water pollution? Choose a body of water near you and get to know it. Where does the water come from? Where does it go? Are there insects, such as mayflies, swarming around, or is the water very still?

Take a water sample and look at it under a microscope. Count the animals, fish, and insects you see living near or in the water. Talk to people living near the water to learn about the water's history. Call your local pollution-control agency to share your findings and solutions. Find out who dumps things in the water, and then make an action plan to make your water healthier.

WETLANDS WISDOM

Students at Dunstan Junior High in Lakeland, Colorado, adopted a 4.4-acre wetland for scientific study. They took water samples and counted the numbers of each type of plant and animal they found. They researched how the wetland helped wildlife and the city itself. They built trails and put up educational signs and nesting boxes for ducks. Now Lakeland citizens can learn about wetlands as they hike.

Land's End?

Don't Dump on Me!

People like to bury garbage where they can't see it. They think if you can't see it, it can't hurt you. But it can. Some garbage is so dangerous it is called toxic. It can burn you, poison you, or cause cancer.

Toxic garbage can come from places such as chemical factories, nuclear-power plants, gas stations, and garbage burners. Sometimes companies and governments try to dump toxic garbage in neighborhoods that aren't rich and fancy. They think the people there won't do anything about the dumping. But they are wrong. People of all ages and places are working together to keep their neighborhoods clean and healthy. They are saying, "Toxic waste should not be dumped in anyone's backyard. If there aren't places to dump it, maybe we should stop making it."

DOWN IN THE DUMPS

In 1987, students at Jackson Elementary in Salt Lake City, Utah, discovered barrels of toxic chemicals dumped in a spot three blocks from their school. With the help of their teacher, the students sent letters to environmental groups, talked to governmental leaders, and got the neighbors involved. A year later the barrels were removed, and the kids made a park on the land.

Power up with Solar

MOTHERS UNITE!

In 1984, California's King County planned to build a burner for toxic wastes in a neighborhood where many people spoke only Spanish. No one thought these people would say anything against the burner. Some women formed the group Mothers of East Los Angeles (MELA). They walked door-to-door, phoned neighbors, and gathered to talk about the danger. The county leaders finally agreed not to build the burner near them. The Mothers of East Los Angeles protected their neighborhood, and they are encouraging other people to do the same thing.

COLD AND BEAUTIFUL

Because the North Pole and the South Pole are so cold, and few people live in these areas, they have not been well protected. Companies drill for oil, and governments do scientific tests, leaving behind pollution. Tourists scatter litter and disturb wildlife. Cruise ships dump their garbage overboard. Hunters kill off whales and seals.

Concerned people worldwide are working to stop the destruction. For more information on the Arctic and Antarctic, write to:

The Antarctica
 Project
7097 D St. SE
Washington, DC
 20003

The International
 Arctic Project
413 Wacouta St.
St. Paul, MN
 55101

NEW WARS AGAINST THE INDIANS?

Ever since Europeans arrived in America, the peoples who first lived here have had to struggle to save their lands. Now there are new struggles going on. Companies have placed toxic dumps or burners near Indian reservations. Army scientists have tested nuclear weapons on or near reservations. Businesses have tried to take away reservation lands for mining, drilling, building, or dam reservoirs. Nations, such as the Hopi, the Chippewa, and the Shoshone, are working to protect their lands.

For up-to-date news on these struggles, listen to "Native News" on public radio stations. Your teacher or class can also order subscriptions of:

Native Monthly Reader
P.O. Box 217
Crestone, CO 81131

Native Nations
175 5th Ave.
Suite 2245
New York, NY
10010

The High Cost of Living

Having dirty land, water,
and air is not new.
Throughout history,
many groups of people have
had trouble living on land
without spoiling it.
Sometimes they didn't know how.
Other times they thought it cost too
much or was too much work
to worry about the earth.
More and more, though,
people are understanding
that it's harder to make a living
in places where the earth
has been spoiled.
Working *with* nature,
rather than against nature,
always costs less in the long run.
In many different countries,
people with very little money
are proving this can be done!

FOREST FARMING

• In Nigeria, farmers are growing crops between trees so they don't have to cut down the forest. Their crops are growing better than ever before. In many other countries people are also combining farming and forestry for healthier crops and lands.

• In areas of the Amazon, people can grow lianas, or tropical vines, right in the rain forest. The oil from lianas can be sold to factories for machines.

OUTDOOR COOKING

Instead of cutting and hauling wood for stoves, many people are letting the sun cook for them. Solar ovens are easy and cheap to build, and they help save the forests.

GRASSLAND GRAINS

In Nepal, villagers cut grasslands in the national parks for grains to make bread. Since the grasses are never plowed over, they keep growing and making new seeds. The villagers always have something to eat, and so do the wild animals.

CHICKEN OF THE TREES

In many places, iguanas are considered a tasty dish. These lizards live in the rain forests of Central America. Because they are hunted for food, they are now in danger of dying out. Farmers in Panama are experimenting with raising wild iguanas in forest areas. This way there are more wild iguanas, more acres of rain forest saved, and more farmers making ends meet.

WILDLIFE BRINGS TOURISTS WHO BRING CASH

• In Kenya, Masai villagers are paid to protect the wildlife in local parks so tourists can come to see them. Both the Masai and the wild animals have had a better life since this program started.

PIG POWER

Some Chinese farmers feed their pigs table scraps and put pig manure onto their fields for fertilizer. The farmers plant trees around their fields and burn bricks made of dried marsh plants for their stoves instead of wood. Since using these conservation methods, the farms have produced more cotton and grains than before, and the forests have grown.

TAKING CARE OF THE EARTH IS GOOD BUSINESS

• The citizens and businesses of Osage, Iowa, together save about 1.2 million dollars a year by using energy conservation measures and energy-efficient appliances.

• By cutting down on waste and pollution, the International 3M Company has saved nearly 500 million dollars from 1975 to 1990. And this is only a small start to what they can do to be a better earth citizen.

• Some Minnesota businesses earn money for their throwaways, such as wooden pallets, lint, rags, food scraps, and plastic buckets. The businesses list their unwanted items and the materials they would like to buy in a catalog called B.A.R.T.E.R. (Businesses Allied to Recycle through Exchange and Reuse). It's like a rummage sale for businesses done through a catalog. BARTER businesses are cutting costs and garbage.

• Restaurants, grocery stores, and airlines are donating uneaten good food to organizations for the hungry and homeless.

What's in a War?

Even if we learn to live,
eat, and work in earthwise ways,
our planet may still be in danger.
Some of the most dangerous
kinds of pollution come from war
and getting ready for war.
Many bombs are so toxic that
they can ruin an area of land
for hundreds of years.
So when weapons are made,
tested, and used,
they cause deadly problems
for the earth and all of us on it.

ATOMIC HORRORS

One disastrous day for the earth was August 6, 1945. The U.S. dropped an atomic bomb on Hiroshima, Japan: 210,000 people were killed, and hundreds of thousands were hurt. Poisons from the bomb spread far and wide, causing cancer and other illnesses for decades.

The atomic bomb brought an end to World War II. But it marked a beginning to the making of nuclear bombs. The bombs tested nowadays are 8 to 40 times stronger and more deadly than the one that was dropped on Hiroshima. To learn about one child's experience in Hiroshima, read Sadako and the Thousand Paper Cranes by Eleanor Coerr.

COSTLY CLEANUP

It will cost the U.S. between 40 and 110 billion dollars to clean up areas where nuclear bombs have been made or tested.

Some island peoples in the Pacific Ocean have been harmed by bomb tests and chemical burnings by armies of the U.S. and France. It would cost an enormous amount of money to clean up the islands and ocean, if it could be done at all. But no one can make the people and other animals who have become sick from the pollution well again.

DESERT STORM

During Desert Storm in 1991, soldiers from many different countries were killed. But that's not all.

Thousands of bombs destroyed plants and animals. Over 80 million barrels of oil were spilled into the Persian Gulf. The spill killed herons, cormorants, and flamingos; turtles, shrimp, and oysters; mangrove trees, sea grasses, and coral reefs. About 600 oil wells were set ablaze. The fires sent up a heavy, black smoke that moved over thousands of miles. These fires burned for months.

The United Nations' Children's Fund (UNICEF) estimates that 70,000 children under the age of five died in 1991 alone as a result of this war.

HEALING IN VIETNAM

The war in Vietnam from 1957 to 1975 destroyed over ½ the area's wetlands, as well as much of its rain forests and croplands. This area of the world, which had once been the home of many rare animals and plants, was nearly ruined.

Since the war, the Vietnamese people have worked hard to bring health back to their land. They've tried to find buried land mines and dig them up. They've dug ditches to bring water back to dried-out areas. They've planted countless trees, and they've made laws against hunting rare animals.

Their work is paying off. Gradually the birds, insects, fish, plants, turtles, and snakes are coming back. The Vietnamese have a saying, "Birds only stay in good lands." The rare eastern sarus crane (a relative of the whooping crane) has returned to Vietnam, and its numbers are slowly growing.

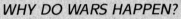

Making Peace

An American army officer, General Omar Bradley, said, "We know more about war than we do about peace, more about killing than we do about living." Many people around the world are tired of what wars have done to us and our planet. They are working to learn more about peaceful living. They study why wars happen, and they experiment with ways to settle arguments that are safer, slower, longer-lasting, and less violent. Each year the Nobel Peace Prize is awarded to someone who has worked to bring about peace. You and your classmates can study the lives of these peace-makers and experiment with peaceful ways to solve arguments.

WHY DO WARS HAPPEN?
Some people and countries do not want to share the earth's natural resources: the land, water, and minerals. Other people and countries want everyone to think and act as they do. Learning to share and to accept other peoples' ways of living, thinking, and believing are two very important ways you can work for peace.

PEACE CAMP FOR KIDS
If you're interested in learning how to be a peace leader, there's a summer peace camp for you. Write to:
    Little Friends for Peace
    4405 29th St.
    Mount Rainier, MD 20712
This organization also has information about how teachers and parents can run their own peace camps.

WAR FREE ZONE

TABLING ARGUMENTS

You and your classmates can try activities that teach you how to work out problems and disagreements. Like world leaders, you can sit down at a Peace Table when you have arguments. Ask a person who is not involved to sit down with you so everyone stays cool. Then you can try talking things out. Each of you can take a turn, telling how you feel and asking questions. Both sides must listen carefully and avoid name-calling or accusing each other. The goal is not to get your way or make a point, but to discover a solution you can both live with. For more ideas and activities about learning peacemaking skills, write to:

Children as
  Peacemakers
950 Battery St.
San Francisco, CA 94111

Children's Creative
  Response to Conflict
P.O. Box 271
Nyack, NY 10960-0271

Friends for a
  Non-Violent World
2025 Nicollet Ave.
Suite 203
Minneapolis,
  MN 55404

VETERANS FOR PEACE

Some of the most powerful peacemakers in the world are soldiers who have survived a war. Many of them are asking their leaders to learn to discuss international problems and find safer ways to solve disagreements. In the U.S., there is a club called Veterans for Peace. Since the 1991 war in the Persian Gulf, more than 1,000 new members have joined.

PEACE THROUGH PARKS

The land and people in Central America have been suffering from war for many years. Some people are trying to start war-free parks along the countries' borders. These parks would protect large sections of rain forest, swamp, and lowland. There are at least 70 of these border parks in the world. One international peace park lies in the Rocky Mountains between the U.S. and Canada.

People Power

The Earth Can Thank Its Children

Sometimes when we hear
about war and pollution,
it may seem like too much.
But there's a lot of good news too.
In countries near and far,
schoolchildren and kids' clubs
are planting trees;
studying animals and plants;
reducing, reusing, and recycling;
working to keep soil in place;
solving problems peacefully;
and cleaning up pollution.
You can be a part of all of this!
Join a group that's already
at work, or start
an earthwise club of your own.

MAKING THE WORLD A CLOSER, GREENER PLANET

When sixth graders from Oak View Elementary near Washington, D.C., traveled to France, they wanted to see what kids there were doing to clean up the planet. So they headed to an environmental camp in Bordeaux. They asked children their age about their earth-saving projects. Other schools around the planet are setting up their own environmental exchange programs. Maybe your student council can get one started at your school.

KID POWER

Young farmers in Thailand plant papaya trees; Girl Scouts in Barbados test the air for pollution; Egyptian children clear streets, alleys, and parks of garbage; youth on the Caribbean island of St. Lucia cut trails in a national park and help lay pipes to bring clean water to villages; elementary school kids in Germany plant shrubs and bushes along streams; kids in the Chongololo and Wildlife Clubs teach conservation to adults. The list of projects accomplished by children is as unending as their imagination and commitment.

If you want to start or join an earthwise club formed by other kids, write to:

Earth Kids Organization
P.O. Box 3847
3898 Commercial St. SE
Salem, OR 07302

Kids Against Pollution
Tenakill School
275 High St.
Closter, NJ 07624

Kids For A Clean
Environment (FACE)
P.O. Box 158254
Nashville, TN 37215

LEADERS' ADVICE

Teachers and parents can get advice on how to lead an environmental club from:

CAKE (Concerns About
   Kids' Environment)
29 Pine St.
Freeport, ME 04032

NatureScope/CLASS Project
National Wildlife Federation
1400 16th St. NW
Washington, DC 20036

KIND (Kids In Nature's
   Defense).
National Association
   for Humane and
   Environmental Education
67 Salem Road
East Haddam, CT 06423

ENVIRONMENTAL AWARDS

Each year students are honored by organizations in their countries or by the United Nations for their earth-saving actions. In the U.S. alone, more than 8,000 young people have applied for the President's Environmental Youth Award in the last two years. For more information about environmental awards, write to:

President's
   Environmental
   Youth Award
Environmental
   Protection Agency
Office of Public Affairs
401 M St. SW, A 108
Washington, DC
   20460

Class Act
Newsweek Inc.
P.O. Box 440
Livingston, NJ
   07039-0440

Cercles des Jeunes
   Naturalistes
4101 Sherbrooke Est
Local 124
Montreal, PQ
CANADA H1X 2B2

Global 500 Award
United Nations
   Environment
   Program (UNEP)
Information and
   Public Affairs
P.O. Box 30552
Nairobi, KENYA

The Community Connection

All around the planet,
kids' groups are finding that
the more they work with
people in their neighborhoods,
the more they get done.
They are urging businesses
to act in more earthwise ways.
They are working with
their governments to make
stronger laws to protect the earth.
They are teaching people
of all ages how to be better
earth citizens.
You can do it too.
Just get your group to get
your community into action!

DOLPHIN DEFENDERS

Tuna companies used to kill dolphins accidentally as they netted tuna. Kids across the continent got mad. They asked their schools to stop serving tuna for lunch. They refused to eat tuna at home. They wrote letters to tuna companies, asking them to fish for tuna in a different way.

The tuna companies got the message. Now many North American tuna companies fish for tuna in a way that doesn't harm dolphins. When the StarKist Company introduced their new dolphin-safe tuna label, they invited two groups of students to the party to thank them for their concern.

SWAMP SAVING
AND OCEAN ACTION

Can students save a cypress swamp?
Or pass a state law to protect bald eagles?
Or set aside an ocean preserve for manatees?
You bet! Students in Lee County, Florida, have done all these things. Since 1969, teenagers have worked with teacher Bill Hammond to save the state's plants and animals. The students choose their project, research the problem, and then get the community involved. It may take them years, but that doesn't stop them. As some students graduate, other students take up the project.

RETURNING TO DEPOSITS

Reusing bottles is even better than recycling them. So students at Ipswich Middle School in Massachusetts wanted a state law requiring that juice and alcoholic beverages be packaged in glass bottles with deposits. The kids started a club called SAVE, Students Against Vandalizing the Earth. They studied the deposit issue and collected signatures from 4,000 people who wanted the deposit law. But alcohol companies urged state legislators not to vote for it.

The students are taking a break from the deposit project to work on a law to reduce extra packaging. They are also planting trees, picking up recyclables from homebound people, raising money for environmental causes, and teaching people about composting.

BE EARTH IMPROVERS!

You and your friends have the power to change the world! For advice on how you can do it, read The Kid's Guide to Social Action by Barbara Lewis. You can find it in the library or at a bookstore.

FREEING UP FREEPORT FROM FOAM

When elementary kids in Freeport, Maine, heard that chemicals used to make foam containers damage the earth's atmosphere, they called scientists to learn how the chemicals work. They examined costs, alternative packaging, garbage buildup, and harm to the atmosphere. They presented their findings and solutions to their city council. The community agreed that better, more earth-friendly packaging could be used. Freeport banned foam, and the children are looking into other ways to clean up their city.

A World View

Since we are all facing the same kinds of problems, we need to keep in touch with other people around the planet. Together, we can share ideas and help in each others' efforts to clean up the earth and make it more healthy for everyone.

46

Where Do We Go from Here?

Now's Your Chance

What are you and your friends going to do about the problems in your school or community? Start putting together an earthwise action plan! Here's an example:

Let's say your school has decided to turn a nearby field into a parking lot. You and your classmates think it would be better to turn the field into a small wildlife park.

First you and your classmates need to research the parking problem: Why does the school need more parking? Assign people to talk to the principal. Then think about other solutions for parking: Could teachers, staff, and other workers be encouraged to take buses instead? To ride bicycles? To share rides? What do other earthwise schools and businesses do? Assign one or two people to look into each option.

The next step is to discuss all your research. What are the good points and bad points of each option: parking lot, more biking, more busing, more ride-sharing. Using this information, come up with the plan for the school that uses the best parts of all your solutions.

Once you have a plan for solving the transportation problem, you can assign group members to look into the idea of a wildlife park. What animals and plants will lose their homes if a parking lot is put in? What wildlife could you attract to the park? Who would build or plant it? Where could you get the materials? Where could you get the tools? Who else could you get to help you in this project? These are the types of questions you would need to research before you could make a park plan.

After you have researched all parts of your plans for transportation and a wildlife park, make a report and present it to your principal and school board. They may have questions or criticisms. If they do, don't give up. Start at the beginning again—do more research, get more people in the community involved, make a new action plan, and come back to them once more.

An Earthwise Action Plan

Here's an outline to organize the first stage of your project:

1 STUDY THE PROBLEM

What is the problem?
Who is involved or interested?
What do the different people need or want, and why?
What is good for the earth? What isn't?
What information do we need?
Where can we find the information?

2 MAKE ASSIGNMENTS

What needs to be done?   Who will do it?
Talk to:
Write to:
Research _____ topic:
Find adults to help with:
Set up meeting with:

3 SHARE REPORTS & BRAINSTORM SOLUTIONS

Come up with as many different earthwise ways to solve the problem as you can.
Don't worry if ideas sound way-out. The wildest ideas often lead to the most ingenious new solutions.
Research ideas.

4 EVALUATE IDEAS

What are the good and bad points of each suggested solution?
Which is the best solution or mix of solutions:
  For the earth?
  To answer different people's needs and wants?
  To work for a long time (years)?
How much does each solution cost at first? Over time?
Which project would you enjoy doing the most?
What research still needs to be done?

5 CHOOSE GOAL & MAKE NEW ACTION PLAN

For more ideas on earthwise projects, read *Earthwise at Home* and *Earthwise at Play.*

44948

j363.7   Lowery, Linda
LOW
          Earthwise at school

$19.95

DATE		
JUN 0 3 1994		
APR 3 0 1996		
APR 1 8 1997		
MAY 0 5 1997		
MAR 3 1 1998		
OCT 2 7 1999		

BAKER & TAYLOR BOOKS